Motion

Orlando Austin New York San Diego Toronto London

Visit *The Learning Site!*
www.harcourtschool.com

How Things Move

Something moving is in motion. Things move in different ways.

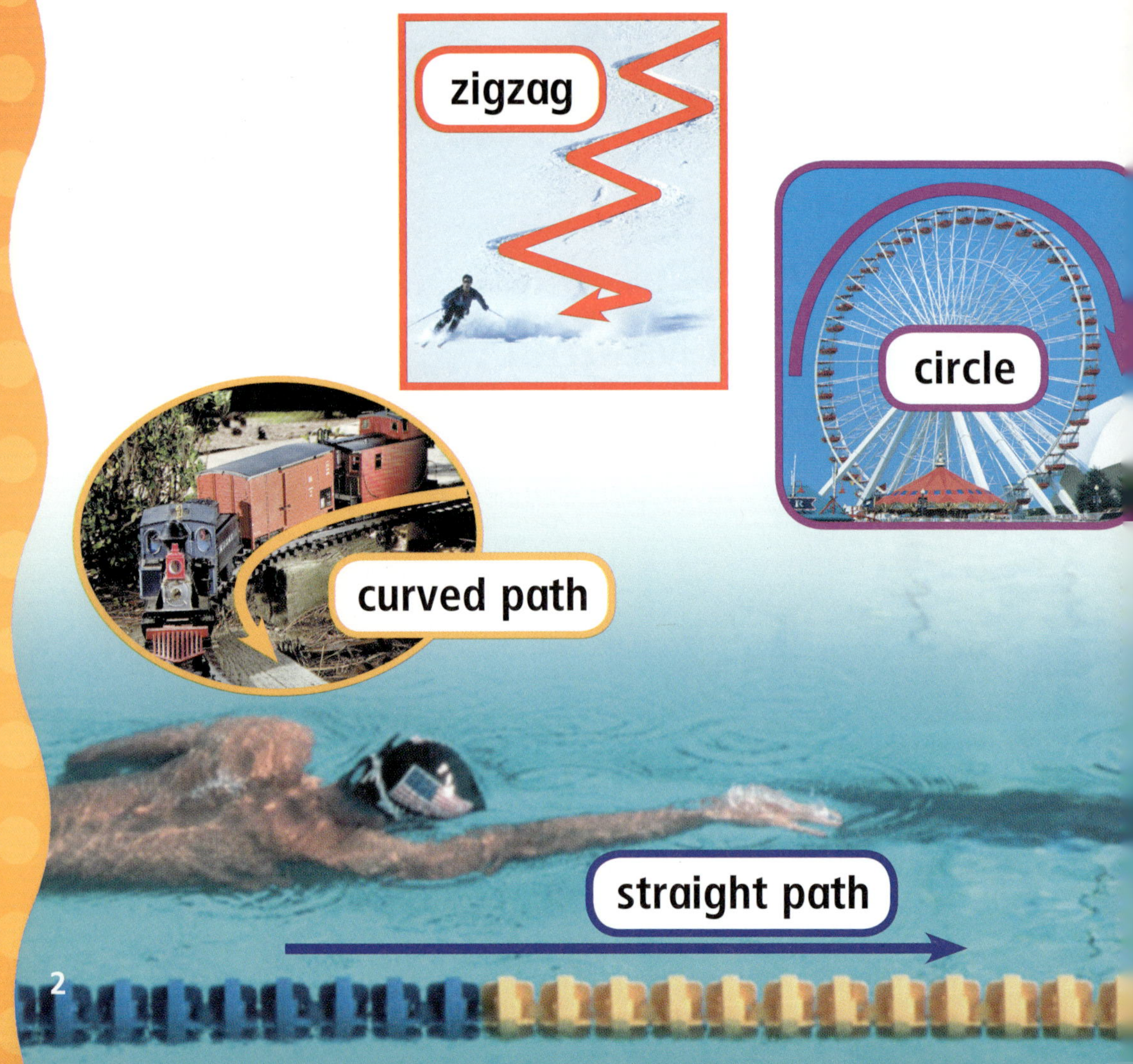

Things move at different speeds. Speed is how fast something moves.

Pushes and Pulls

A force makes things move or stop. Pushes and pulls are forces.

You push something away from you.
You pull something toward you.

Using Force

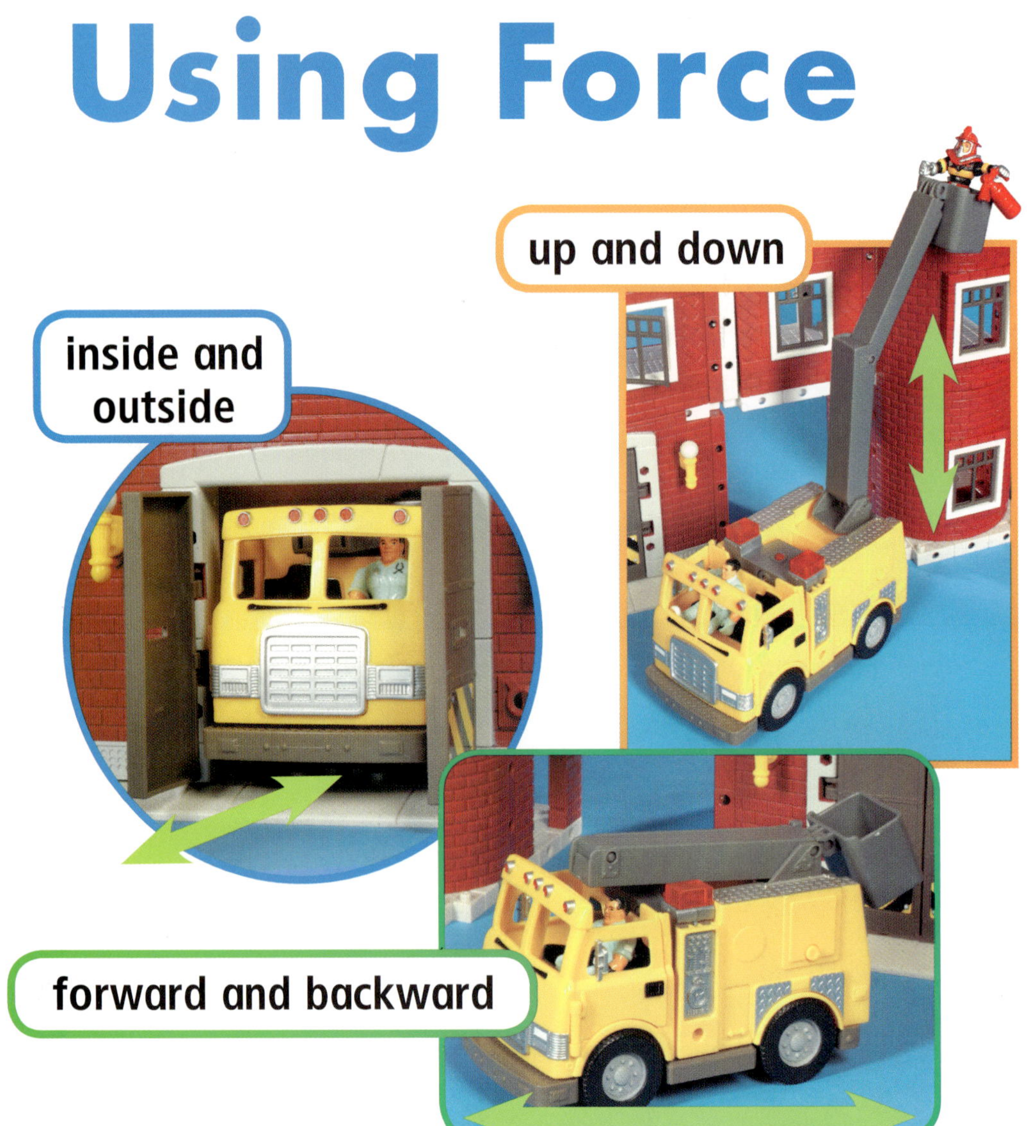

You can use force to change things. Force can change where an object is.

The batter changes the ball's direction.

It can change an object's direction.
It can also change an object's speed.

Gravity

Gravity pulls the girl down the slide.

Gravity is a force.
It pulls things down to the ground.

Magnets

A magnet attracts things made of iron. Its pull is called magnetic force.

Poles of a Magnet

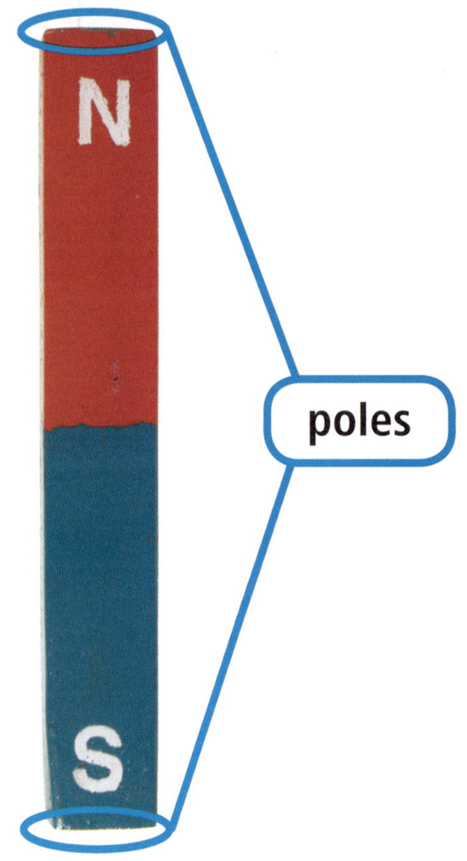

Magnets have a pole at each end.
The pull is strongest at the poles.

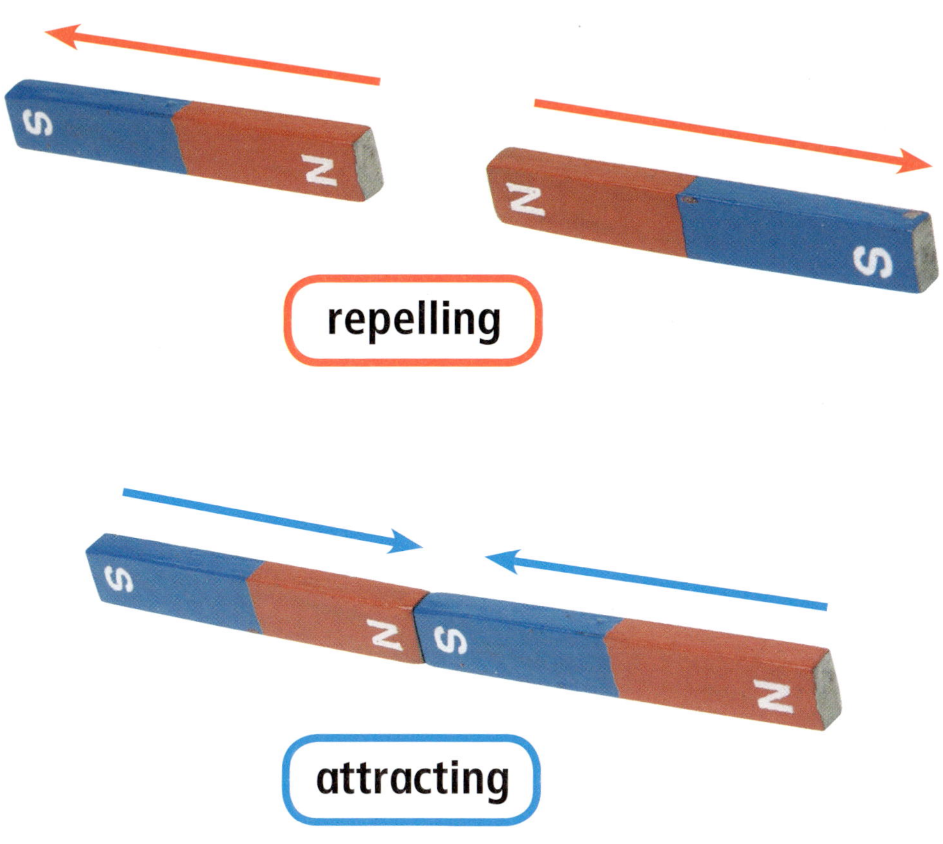

Different poles attract each other.
Like poles repel, or push each other away.

Vocabulary